THE DISMISSIVE AVOIDANT ATTACHMENT STYLE & HOW CHILDHOOD TRAUMAS CAN RESULT IN DYSFUNCTIONAL BEHAVIORS IN ADULT RELATIONSHIPS

(Learn Your Triggers & Begin to Heal)

LEVER AGE 4 CHANGE

CHRISTINE CHIN-SIM, PH.D., M.B.A

Leverage4change Coaching & Consulting, LLC
www.leverage4change.com

Dedication

This book is dedicated to my Lord and Savior Jesus Christ. Without Him, I can do nothing. With Him, I can do ALL things as He continues to strengthen me.
(Philippians 4:13)

Please note: When listening, please keep in mind that not all individuals with this attachment style will exhibit all the traits or behaviors expressed. Every attachment style is always along a spectrum and every individual is different. This book can only provide you with the groundwork for becoming aware of your attachment style or your partner's, so you can begin the journey of healing to become a more secure individual - which is a necessary component for having healthy, secure relationships.

Table of Contents

WHY I WROTE THIS BOOK

As a relationship and life coach, I've seen my fair share of broken and toxic relationships and the common threads that seem to run through them.

I've also had my own personal experiences in my relationships, and having studied Marriage & Family Therapy in my doctoral studies; my combined experiences now serve to form a strong base from which I help individuals struggling in the inter (relationship with others), and intra-personal (relationship with self) relationships.

I approach my work primarily from the perspective of Attachment Styles, as I've found that the ways in which a child connected with their caregivers, now form the subconscious base from which they now experience relationships as adults.

My goal for this book, is to equip individuals with the basic knowledge of the role their attachment style plays in their adult relationships and how they can begin the journey of healing from, and changing their subconscious patterns of behavior that currently wreak havoc in their relationships

I wanted to make is as simple as possible; no academic jargon, just useable information to help inform and create changes.

My hope is that this information will serve to reduce the challenges and traumas individuals face as they navigate their relationship and life challenges.

INTRODUCTION

If we've lived long enough, we will find that relationships can be quite a challenge.

As a relationship coach, I've seen firsthand how entrenched ways of behaving in relationships, can result in toxic and unhealthy relationships. These unhealthy relationships can leave one or both partners bruised and battered from chronic emotional abuse.

Many tell the same story: "This person was so nice and romantic at the beginning and now I don't even recognize who this person is."

Others enter relationships, even when they recognize early on in the dating period, that a relationship with this individual would not make them happy.

Many find themselves, having the same type of relationship with different partners and finding themselves asking, "Why do I keep attracting the same man/woman over and over again?"

Many go from one relationship to the other, finding that as soon as the object of their affection whom they pursued with such ferocity appear to reciprocate similar feelings of attraction, they get bored, or become so uncomfortable with the emotional closeness that they begin to feel suffocated and trapped.

Why does this happen?

Happily, there is an explanation.

As children, we experienced our relationship with our caregivers in different ways.

These experiences dictated how we attach to our caregivers, and how we now respond in our adult relationships - especially romantic ones.

I won't be going in depth concerning Attachment Theory or the different attachment styles that have been discovered as a result of extensive research; however, I want to at least introduce you to them, in an effort to give you a broad perspective of each attachment style.

There are four (4) attachment styles. Below are short descriptions outlining the causes and resulting attachment of the child to their caregivers.

- **Anxious Preoccupied (Ambivalent attachment)** These children become very distressed when a parent leaves. As a result of inconsistency in parental availability, these children could not depend on their primary caregiver to be there when they need them. They can become clingy and anxious when they are not close to their loved ones. This is particularly evident in very close relationship, such as romantic ones. The resulting effect from a partner of this attachment style, is to feel suffocated by the constant need for validation and being in close proximity to their partner, both physically and emotionally.

- **Dismissive Avoidant Attachment:** Children with an avoidant attachment tend to avoid parents or caregivers, showing no preference between a caregiver and a complete stranger. This attachment style might be a result of abusive or neglectful caregivers. Children who are punished for relying on a caregiver will learn to avoid seeking help in the future. There was also a lack of emotional connection from the caregiver. Any show of emotions by the child would provoke criticism, rejection or both. The child grows up to feel ashamed for needing emotional validation, and learned not to ask for, or expect it from their caregivers.

- **Fearful Avoidant (Disorganized attachment)**: These children display a confusing mix of behavior, seeming disoriented, dazed, or confused. They may avoid or resist the parent. Lack of a clear attachment pattern is likely linked to inconsistent caregiver behavior. In such cases, parents may serve as both a source of comfort and fear, leading to disorganized behavior. The child's environment may have been very tumultuous, with lots of arguing, abuse, neglect, among others. As a child, they recognize that the source of their survival was also the source of their pain, and learned very early to read any signal from their caregivers, to determine when it might be safe to approach or when it was best to retreat for their survival.

- **Secure attachment**: Children who can depend on their caregivers, show distress when separated and joy when reunited. Although the child may be upset, they feel assured that the caregiver will return. When frightened, securely attached children are comfortable seeking reassurance from caregivers. Care and attention were consistent. These children got a lot of hugs, kisses, validation, and emotional connection from their caregivers. As a result, they learned that relationships were safe and they could trust that they could ask for help when they needed it.

As you can imagine, the securely attached child will have a better chance of success in life and relationships as they grew into adulthood. Research suggests that failure to form secure attachments early in life can have a negative impact on behavior as the child gets older and throughout their adult life.

Early attachments appear to have a serious impact on later relationships. Adults who were securely attached in childhood tend to have good self-esteem, strong sense of self-worth, the ability to ask for the help they need, and the ability to trust and be vulnerable with others. These children also tend to be more independent and self-sufficient – while recognizing their need for others. They perform better in school and later in their careers, have successful intimate, work, and social relationships, and experience less depression and anxiety compared to those with the avoidant or anxious attachment styles.

In this book, I will be focusing on the Dismissive Avoidant Attachment Style, and how this style of attachment now dictates how this individual interacts with their significant others in romantic relationships. Although this attachment style affects every relationship, the effects are magnified in romantic relationships because of the lack of emotional intelligence and depth this type of attachment style is challenges with.

WHAT IS ATTACHMENT THEORY?

Attachment theory is based on how we interacted with parents and caregivers as children, and the causes for how these children attached to their caregivers can be traced back to a very young age.

Attachment theory outlines the characteristic way people relate to others in the context of relationships. The degree of attachment security in adults is directly related to how children bonded to their caregivers early in their childhood. It describes a special relationship that involves an exchange of emotional proximity to caregivers, degree of care, and a child's trust that caregivers will be there when they need them.

BOWLBY'S RESEARCH FINDINGS

John Bowlby devoted extensive research to the concept of attachment, describing it as a "lasting psychological connected-ness" between human beings. He proposed that early experiences in childhood are important for influencing development and behavior later in their adult life and relationships.

In addition to this, Bowlby believed that the attachment the child formed with their caregivers was in response to their survival instinct which is always working to protect them. For example, a child who was constantly ignored or shamed for any emotional expression, would soon learn to stop trying to connect with their caregivers, and instead find a way of soothing and providing for their own emotional needs.

At an innate level, children seek this emotional bond because they understand that their caregivers provide everything they need for their survival, and that strong emotional bonds to particular individuals, is a strong component for what humans need to survive.

Bowlby believed that there are four distinguishing characteristics of attachment:

- **Proximity maintenance**: The desire to be near the people we are attached to.

- **Safe haven**: The ability to return to the attachment figure for comfort and safety in the face of a fear or threat.
- **Secure base**: The attachment figure acts as a base of security from which the child can explore the surrounding environment.
- **Separation distress**: The anxiety that occurs in the absence of the attachment figure.

He made three key propositions about attachment theory. First, he suggested that when children are raised with confidence that their primary caregiver will be available to them, they are less likely to experience fear than those who are raised without such conviction.

Secondly, he believed that this confidence is forged during a critical period of development, during the years of infancy, childhood, and adolescence. The expectations that are formed during that period tend to remain relatively unchanged for the rest of the individual's life and are directly tied to the child's experience with their caregiver.

AINSWORTH'S CONTRIBUTION | THE "STRANGE SITUATION"

In the 1970s, Mary Ainsworth, a psychologist, further expanded upon Bowlby's work with her study titled, "a strange situation." This study revealed the profound effects of attachment on a child's behavior later in life.

In this study, researchers observed children between the ages of 12 and 18 months as they responded to a situation in which they were briefly left alone and then reunited with their mothers.

Based on the responses the researchers observed, Ainsworth described three major styles of attachment: secure attachment, ambivalent-insecure attachment, and avoidant-insecure attachment.

Later, researchers Main and Solomon (1986) added a fourth attachment style called disorganized-insecure attachment based on their own research.

A number of studies since then have supported Ainsworth's attachment styles and have indicated that attachment styles also have an impact on how adults showed up and experienced relationships later in life.

Although these attachment styles will have an impact on all relationships; intimate or romantic relationships are usually the most challenging because of the emotional closeness and proximity expected and required.

In this book, I will be focusing on the Dismissive Avoidant Attachment Style. Below is a brief description on how this particular attachment style is formed.

The dismissive-avoidant attachment is formed when a baby or small child doesn't get the physical care or emotional attention they need from their parents or caregivers. In turn, the infant or child learns that expressing their needs wouldn't guarantee that they will be taken care of, and learns to find other ways to soothe themselves.

As a result, they learn to be very self-reliant and independent of the need to depend on others. They learned very early, that if they needed to get something done or wanted something, they had to do it, or get it themselves.

CHILDHOOD EXPERIENCE

Children with avoidant attachment styles tend to avoid parents and caregivers because the recurring experience was one of neglect and rejection. This tangible expression of avoidance often becomes especially pronounced after a period of absence by the caregiver. This child may not even look up to acknowledge the parent when they eventually return to the room.

While they may not outrightly reject attention from a parent or caregiver, these children might not seek out comfort or contact from them. Children with an avoidant attachment show no preference between a parent and a complete stranger, because there was never an emotional connection between child and caregiver.

As Children

- Child may avoid parents as much as possible
- They do not seek much contact or comfort from parents
- Show little or no preference for parents over strangers
- Learned to self-soothe so they don't depend on caregivers to soothe them
- Always felt alone even when caregivers are nearby

- Learned to entertain themselves for hours
- May not cry even if they hurt themselves because they knew from experience that nobody was coming to help them – if a stranger tried to help – they may feel uncomfortable and say they are okay.
- Usually a loner – very limited social skills
- Any attempt at emotional responses appears robotic and inauthentic
- Dislike physical touch and will freeze when unexpectedly touched or held.

As Adults

- You may have problems with intimacy – physical and emotional
- You may invest little emotional energy in social and romantic relationships
- You may be unwilling or unable to share your thoughts or feelings with others
- You get overwhelmed if emotional expression is expected of you, for example, going over to express condolences to someone who just lost a loved one.
- You may choose your space over a relationship, and if/when a relationship ends, may show little signs of distress.
- You may use your work commitments as excuses to avoid intimacy (working overtime, weekends, or volunteer for work travel for extended periods etc.,).
- You may be uncomfortable making eye contact

- You may fantasize about other people during sex.
- Research has also shown that adults with an avoidant attachment style may be more accepting of, and more likely to engage in casual sex.
- You may fail to support partners during stressful times and find it difficult and uncomfortable to share feelings, thoughts, and emotions with your partners.
- You may have difficulty being around people who show vulnerability, as well as, difficulty expressing vulnerability.
- You tend to idealize past relationships which keeps current partner at a distance. This happens when you begin to feel emotionally overwhelmed or suffocated by your partner.

CAREGIVER'S PROFILE

Parents or caregiver can be a single mom or dad, may be addicted to drugs or alcohol, may suffer from depression, is overworked. Caregivers may also have learned their behavior from their parents when they were children, and the problem just continued to the next generation. Different variations of caregivers could be foster parents, grandparents, both parents (mom and dad) or any variation of these.

The important component to remember is that, emotional expression was not welcomed, valued, or tolerated.

These caregivers may not have mirrored their child's facial expressions and was extremely inconsistent with their care. Face-to-face time, was most likely non-existent, and no time was spent just playing with child and looking into their eyes for no other reason than to show them love.

Another important component that is integral to the growth of a secure child is skin- to-skin contact (hugs, kisses, caresses, touch), which was either minimal or completely nonexistent. Any type of connection initiated by the caregiver would be purposeful. For example – to teach the child a task (to feed themselves, to tie their shoe laces, etc. This basic connection (two individuals sharing a close space only for the purpose of performing or teaching a task) was only attempted for success in task-based activities. Emotions were not expressed during these tasks (except perhaps anger or criticism at the child for not completing the task properly). These children were rarely validated or encouraged.

This chronic shame, criticism and lack of physical or emotional connection led to stunted emotional development for the child. Later in life, they struggle to express, empathize, or understand the emotional expressions of those around them.

The caregiver is usually busy doing their own thing and the child is usually left alone to entertain themselves. Although the caregiver may provide the basics for survival – food, clothing, shelter; they failed to take time to listen, validate or coregulate any emotional outbursts the child may suffer, and can be very harsh with their shaming, criticism, and punishment when the child fails to live up to their standard of perfection.

ATTACHMENT PROFILE QUIZ

**If You Answer "Yes" to These Questions –
You Have a Dismissive Avoidant Attachment Style.**

Question 1
I need a lot of space and get upset when others try   (Yes/No)
to take that from me.

Question 2
I don't understand the hype about being in touch   (Yes/No)
with my emotions. I feel I get along quite well
without them.

Question 3
I frequently experience inward emotional turbu-   (Yes/No)
lence throughout the duration of my romantic and
close family or friend relationships.

Question 4
I often fluctuate around how I feel towards my   (Yes/No)
partner or family members. I tend to operate in
extremes in how I relate to others.

Question 5

If someone hurt me, I often have a strong fight or flight response. I want to get as far away from them as possible.   (Yes/No)

Question 6

I do not depend on others to fulfill my emotional or other needs. I find it difficult to understand why others need me to meet their needs when I am always able to meet my own needs.   (Yes/No)

Question 7

Commitment to set plans made by others makes me uncomfortable. I feel cornered and trapped.   (Yes/No)

Question 8

Setting boundaries comes naturally to me. I prefer to keep others out of my space.   (Yes/No)

Question 9

I am very protective over my privacy and belongings. Truth be told, I would give up a relationship if it impinges on my ability to have my privacy.   (Yes/No)

Question 10

I generally feel overwhelmed and my personal space compromised, when my partner, friends or family members demand too much physical affection from me.   (Yes/No)

CORE WOUNDS OF
THE DISMISSIVE AVOIDANT

Fear of abandonment: Because of chronic emotional neglect – limited or no skin-to-skin contact, hugs, kisses, limited or no eye contact, loving touches, caregiver speaking lovingly to child) these individuals always have a fear that their caregivers may abandon them, because they felt they were not loved or valued.

Fear of criticism – Easily misunderstood because they have difficulty expressing how they feel or have conversations around how to solve problems. Because they never learned how to coregulate with others to solve problems, they learned very early were they had to solve it themselves. They learned to self-regulate by self-soothing activities. For example, as children, they could sit for hours playing by themselves: now as adults, they may use other activities such as, excessive gaming, pornography, one-night stands, excessive TV watching, dangerous hobbies, long work hours etc. These activities do not require any emotional commitment and they use them to stem the real pain of low self-worth and loneliness they often feel.

Lack of trust in relationships: They could not trust their caregivers to be there for them when they needed them. As a result, they feel safer connecting with inanimate objects (may collect certain items – for example, paintings, collectibles, may have pets, since they do not require emotional commitment (while fulfilling the need for love and connection they so desperately need).

I am unworthy of love: Feels defective; since as a child they felt something must be really wrong with them for their parents not to want to hug, kiss or cuddle them or care for their emotional needs. They feel (at a subconscious level) that if they keep others from getting too close, they will not find out who they really are (somehow deficient in some way, so that even their parents/caregivers could not love them).

I am powerless: As children they felt powerless at the hands of their caregivers because they did not have the power to do anything about their situation. As a result, when faced with too much emotion as adults – there is a great feeling of anxiety and overwhelm, and a sense of being trapped or suffocated.

I am alone: As children they felt alone, even when parents or caregivers were in the same room. This made them feel unloved and unsupported. This forced them to learn how to soothe and satisfy their own needs

HOW THE DISMISSIVE AVOIDANT ATTACHEMENT STYLE SHOWS UP IN RELATIONSHIPS

Being independent and teaching your children how to be independent, is extremely important for survival. Unfortunately, having a dismissive-avoidant attachment style is not ideal for relationships, and the individual with this attachment style may negatively affect, both the happiness of the person with this attachment style, as well as those close to them.

1. They do not trust relationships. While most individuals feel safer when they are connected to others. This isn't the case for someone with dismissive avoidant attachment; they might actually feel safer keeping their distance. For someone with this attachment style, deep emotional attachments make them feel anxious, suffocated, and caged.

2. One of the major complaints of partners of a dismissive-avoidant attachment style, is that their emotional needs are minimized or completely ignored by their partner.

3. Because this individual seeks solitude more often than most. He/she may pick fights, flirt with others, etc., – to start a quarrel, just so they can have an excuse to be alone.

4. Usually avoid shows of affection – hugs, holding hands, eye contact, kisses, physical touch etc., may even grudgingly agree to a somewhat lukewarm show of affection at your request, then ask, "Are you satisfied now?"- as if doing you a favor.

5. Difficulty having conversations that may enter into the realm of emotional expressions. The usual response is to shut down and distance themselves at any sign of conflict.

6. There is difficulty expressing themselves in terms of emotions – uses logic instead. As a result, partners of this attachment style may feel they are speaking two different languages, since they fail to connect emotional concerns with someone who only understands logic.

7. This attachment style is prone to be workaholics and usually excel at what they do. This is because they are more committed to work, than their relationships.

8. It's best not to expect empathy, since this attachment style finds it difficult to understand how others feel.

9. They are quite willing to do things for their partner; however, they have difficulty asking for help themselves. They prefer not to ask others for any help. They fear being obligated to others and feel obligated to return the favor if someone does something for them before they had the chance to refuse the help.

10. Frequently feels misunderstood by their partner because the dismissive avoidant individual rarely shares their feelings or their needs.

11. Another common complaint of their loved ones is that they feel neglected. Partners, close friends, and family members

of someone with a dismissive-avoidant attachment style can also feel deprived of emotional connection or closeness and feel that their basic need for emotional connection goes unmet in the relationship. They feel disconnected and neglected, and even when in the presence of their dismissive avoidant partner, they tend to feel completely alone.

12. Can be very charming at the beginning of relationships (dating) but cannot maintain that charm for long.

13. Very cagey about their personal life – family, work, plans. Asking questions about their personal life makes them uncomfortable and if they do respond, will only give you surface, logic-based responses

14. Will not make concrete plans in advance – which will have you wondering whether you will see them and when – creates a lot of anxiety in partner. (Designed to keep you at a certain distance).

15. Very slow to move relationship forward, especially after initial meeting where they made you feel they wanted a relationship. This can leave their partners feeling confused about their intentions.

16. You never quite know what to expect or where you stand in the relationship. Feels like you are always a second-thought – not a priority. Prioritizes work and their independence over anything to do with you, and may actually tell you that they need their space and can't be with someone who is "needy." May even suggest you spend time and do things with your friends (which is healthy – however, this is not balanced with time they want to spend with you). They basically want you to

live your own life – so they can also live theirs. However, they may want to be able to pop in whenever they want and expect you to be available (unfortunately – someone with the anxious avoidant style will happily concede to this request even when they feel like an after-thought).

17. There's a sense that there's an invisible wall beyond which you cannot go. You feel that you only know this individual from a surface level. They don't open up about their personal struggles because they feel they cannot depend on anyone but themselves to fix it.

18. The dismissive avoidant individual despises small talk – which can be anything that is not logic or task-based. Having a conversation for the sake of bonding or strengthening emotional closeness is not welcomed. Communication for this attachment style is primarily to give information or discuss solutions to problems. They will probably say, "Just get to the point."

19. Can get distant when they feel emotionally overwhelmed. This can be particularly painful when this happens after a wonderful date. For you – it made you feel emotionally closer – for the dismissive avoidant, the emotional depth was beyond what they can tolerate.

20. Can be very rigid. Not very open to trying new things as this would disturb their need for control over their life. Trying new things requires a certain amount of vulnerability since making mistakes are a part of trying anything new. This makes them feel stupid and they don't like feeling stupid. Making mistakes as a child would be met with criticism from their caregivers - causing them to feel shamed and stupid. Now as adults, they

attempt to control their environment by creating routine around many of their behaviors, so they can feel safer.

21. As a general rule – they are very sensitive to any indication of criticism – even when it wasn't meant that way. They will most likely not approach you if they felt you've hurt their feelings or disrespected them in some way. Instead, they will shut down or disappear. Instead, they may become very spiteful and withhold affection to punish you – but they won't approach you to resolve the matter.

22. You feel you cannot count on your partner with this attachment style. They avoid any bid for intimacy and you never feel secure that they will be there for the long haul.

23. Very private when it comes to introducing and incorporating you into their family, friends, and work-related circle even after years of dating.

24. Their speech is more about logic–based because they find it difficult to express emotions in conversations.

25. Any physical or emotional closeness makes the dismissive avoidant partner very uncomfortable. Hugs, physical touch, eye contact, holding hands – appear robotic and unnatural.

26. Home or personal space will reflect a coldness this person embodies. It is unlikely that you will see photographs of family members, friends, of you or those close to them displayed in their personal space. Soft cushions, colorful throw blankets, paintings, that warms a space will be missing. Might not be open to allow you to leave anything if you stay at their house – which is usually discouraged. They don't want you to start getting too comfortable in their space.

27. The closest you can expect in terms of emotional expression is restrained anger. Even happiness or joy seems restrained and dulled.

28. Uncomfortable with show of emotions – laughing too loud, excitable communication, expressions of sadness or joy – was probably shamed by caregivers if they expressed any type of emotion. Will try to manage your emotional expressions like shushing you when you get too excited over something.

29. Seem deliberate in their intentions to keep you at a distance. (May walk ahead of you – sometimes refusing to hold your hand if you try to hold theirs, sit on a different couch or chair when in the same room. May insist on keeping their home – even after marriage, since they want to have somewhere to escape to when things get uncomfortable. Will change subject if conversation has any emotional depth (disagreements – planning your future together, a concern you may have).

30. Will find way to put you down by criticizing what you wear – how you speak, how you laugh, talk – many times will say they're joking. This is a strategy meant to keep you emotionally at a distance.

31. Is usually fiercely independent, and sees that as a great attribute. However, this is only a cover for the low self-worth and their need to prove they don't need anyone.

32. A relationship with a dismissive avoidant can feel like one step forward – and 2 steps backwards. You never quite know where you stand.

PATTERNS OF BEHAVIOR:
HOW TO DETERMINE IF YOU HAVE THIS
ATTACHMENT STYLE

1. You find the behaviors of others who play the victim very annoying and distasteful, because you believe that people should take responsibility for their own problems.

2. You create boundaries that limit their access to your personal & professional life and will not be open to introducing partners to your family/friends; neither are you interested in meeting theirs. You are unlikely to invite partners to work functions or events, even when the invitation permits; and the excuse you will give is that you are a very private person and don't need people in your business. You may also be flippant about it and say – it will happen when it happens – what's the rush? Any connection to others is usually at a surface level.

3. You consider showcasing personal photos as frivolous and unnecessary and is not one to display your pic, your partner's pic, or the pics of family members or friends in your personal space. You are very protective of your privacy and having people question you about photos, is not something you want to encourage.

4. You're not open to allowing those you're in relationship with to leave anything in your home. You don't want them to start getting too comfortable in your space, which will infringe on your privacy.

5. You view conflict as a threat and will either disengage, or leave, because of your lack of emotional vulnerability.

6. You suppress your emotions and see vulnerability as a sign of weakness. You learned to hide and suppress emotional expression as they were seen as weakness by your caregivers. As a result, you now see those who express emotions as weak and look down on others who express need for emotional connection. You see other's need for emotional or physical connection as needy or clingy.

   You feel safer keeping intense emotions to yourself, since you were ridiculed for any emotional expression as a child.

7. Your conversations are usually surface level without any emotional depth. They are usually short, logical, task or project-based. Conversations for you is to fulfill a purpose and you find wordy conversations annoying and a waste of your time. As a result, you become very impatient with those who have the tendency to ramble on.

8. You prefer to solve problems on your own instead of asking for, or accepting help. You feel you need to take care of everything yourself – as you feel you are on your own – even when in a relationship. You do not want to be a burden to others. Instead of asking for help, you learn to focus on how to fix the problems yourself.

9. You have no problem helping others but find it difficult to accept help from others. You dislike feeling indebted to anyone.

10. You become distant when angry but will rarely show emotions – except for restrained anger on rare occasions.

11. You're are very protective of your privacy, time and space – and if given a choice, you will choose your privacy over a relationship, even when you love your partner or spouse.

12. You need to feel in control of your life and will create routine activities and schedules to accomplish that. You find it difficult to be spontaneous. This can make you seem very rigid to others.

13. You prefer to live alone because you feel you cannot control the behavior of others and you need to be in control of your environment as much as possible.

14. You find it difficult to understand how to be emotionally vulnerable. It's hard for you to relate to others when they show vulnerability. As a result, self-awareness is difficult to achieve.

15. You retreat when someone criticizes or hurt you. Your tendency is to withdraw to deal with what has happened. You won't usually seek out the person who hurt you to resolve the problem because you dislike confrontations and difficult, emotionally based conversations. Criticism is your kryptonite and you distance yourself quickly from the whomever does this to you.

16. You are very protective of your peace – which basically means no type of uncomfortable conversations – you may respond to someone's concern by telling them what they want to hear to relieve any tension. Or you may simply distance from the situation by leaving the vicinity.

17. Because you've always made important decisions on your own as a child – you enter adult relationships expecting to do the same; not recognizing that as a couple, both parties should do this together. Partners see this as controlling because you will want your partner to simply fall in line with the decisions you've made.

18. You can be (at a logical level) attracted to individuals who have their own stuff together and are independent – however, you might be dealing with another avoidant person – and there is difficulty making a connection with someone who has the same core wounds as you do.

19. However, your greatest tendency is usually an intense attraction to the anxiously attached individual. Their expressions of emotions make them seem fun and alive: and these are missing in your life. Sadly, this becomes intolerable for you later on in the relationship, because their emotional expressions become too much for you to handle.

20. You see yourself as independent and the tendency is to look down on others who you see as needy and weak. Uses a façade of independence and self-sufficiency as cover up for deep feelings of unworthiness, because you felt you were inadequate in some way since you didn't feel loved or wanted by your caregiver

21. When you want to distance, you tend to focus on your partner's faults and perceived imperfections, bring up the glorious attributes of a past partner, or pick fights as a way of distancing yourself from your partner/spouse.

22. You like when others depend on you for material things or help in some physical way; but emotional dependency is usually rebuffed.

23. You are often secretive and rigid, not allowing your own plans to be influenced by others and, often, not even disclosing those plans unless completely necessary.

24. Often more prone to short and shallow romantic partnerships, in which the connection is casual and is usually short-lived. This helps you avoid any feelings of closeness to others, and you won't offer others the opportunity to feel close to you.

25. You are usually a great provider, and will be there to fix something, solve a problem - but when it comes to soothing someone who's had a difficult day – been hurt in some way – your discomfort with expressions of emotions comes into play and you basically freeze or retreat.

WHAT YOU NEED TO BE HAPPY

Dismissive Avoidants in Relationships

1. Harmony – where relationship flows easily without any problems (those requiring show of emotions).
2. Free to come and go as you please
3. Consistency – predictability – control over your time and how you use it
4. Partner should be emotionally independent – since you don't want to feel responsible for meeting emotional the needs of your partners.
5. Humor – banter – fun (for you). Usually at the expense of someone else's discomfort.
6. Encouragement and validation – but not too much to come off as inauthentic
7. Drama -free environment
8. Believes absence makes the heart grow fonder – and each person should have their space and do their own thing (which might be too much for the other attachment styles – specifically the anxious preoccupied).
9. Privacy must be respected.
10. Time alone – not to be questioned

WHAT IS EMOTIONAL INTELLIGENCE?

The Dismissive Avoidant & Emotional Intelligence

Emotional intelligence is our ability to recognize and understand emotions in ourselves and others, and the ability to use this awareness to manage our behaviors and relationships.

Emotions can help us and they can hurt us, and until we understand them, it's like walking into each life situation with blinders on.

Although we all experience multiple episodes of emotions daily, most of us are not aware of them. We become aware only when the emotions we feel, dictate how we react to certain triggers.

It makes sense then, that the first step to becoming more in tune with our emotions, is that we first become aware of them, as well as the stimuli that triggers them.

Because the caregivers of the Dismissive Avoidant did not encourage their child to experience and process their emotions, this attachment style now find themselves at a deficit, and respond to emotions by stifling, stuffing, or burying them so deep in their subconscious, that interacting with others in relationships or social activities becomes a difficult experience.

All emotions are made of five core feelings: anger, fear, shame, sadness and happiness. Every waking hour of our lives, we are subjected to a barrage of emotions. Many of these emotions operate just beyond our awareness and in order to bring them forth, we must deliberately become more aware of our emotions and the triggers that hijack our emotions.

This will take time, effort, and consistency. If you think about it; most of us have been operating in the same way to particular emotional triggers all our lives. These thought patterns which bring on certain emotions have been hard-wired into our subconscious (through repetition, emotion and consistency) and now drive our embedded subconscious patterns of behavior.

Our emotions have become so wired to a specific response, that we now act before we even realize what we are doing. The first step to changing these patterns of behaviors is to become aware of the emotions behind them and the meaning we have given these emotions, which is usually connected to our past experiences.

HOW TO DEVELOP EMOTIONAL INTELLIGENCE

Self-Awareness

Self-awareness begins when you are able to accurately recognize our emotions as they are happening, how you tend to respond to these emotions, and why you currently respond the way we do.

Self-awareness is not an easy task, but it is the first step to developing the emotional intelligence you need to be successful in your relationship with others.

Self-awareness can be challenging – especially for the Dismissive Avoidant Attachment style individual, because it requires that you are willing to tolerate the emotional discomfort of negative and painful feelings this exercise will stir up. It requires the ability to accurately perceive your emotions as they occur and understand why you react the way you do in different situations.

Emotions always come from somewhere, and leaning into them and becoming more aware of what is causing them, will put you on the road to more successfully manage them.

Journaling is a great way to do this. Whenever we write things down, we are making that "thing" more tangible. When we have it just floating around in our heads all the time; it is difficult to grab a hold of it and make sense of it.

Writing, in and of itself, brings it to the part of the brain (pre-frontal cortex) where you can make sense of your emotions, dissect, and process them, to see what thoughts or stimuli served as a trigger to bring them forward. When you know that – you can begin to choose more healthy ways of responding to those triggers by replacing old patterns with new ones - every time they occur.

It's this consistent pattern of replacing old toxic patterns of behaviors, with new healthy patterns of behaviors, that will wire these new (healthy) patterns into the subconscious. With consistency and effort, you will soon discover that your past toxic ways of responding to your emotions, now becomes less and less, until the old patterns of behaviors are completely replaced or overwritten.

Once you begin replacing old toxic patterns of behavior, with new healthy patterns, you are now more in control of how you respond to the emotions that were stirred up.

More "in control" means that you are now able to decide how you respond, when you respond, if you respond, which means that you are no longer at the mercy of your emotions. This requires personal competence, which is the ability to stay aware of your emotions and manage subsequent behavior.

I'm not going to sugar-coat it and tell you that this will be an easy process, nothing worth having comes easy. So it's best to take it in small bites, until you build up tolerance for these new ways of thinking and responding.

WHY HEALING CAN BE CHALLENGING | BUT – POSSIBLE

If you have the dismissive avoidant attachment style, you can be quite unaware of why others describe you as cold, distant, and uncaring, etc.,

Instead, your tendency is to mistake yourself for being secure. You believe this because you are able to handle your own emotional states (which is usually by burying it or using artificial ways to push it away: drugs, pornography, excessive gaming, one-night stands, overwork). You fail to recognize that secure individuals have the ability to recognize when they need help, and also the ability to be vulnerable and ask for the help they need. Your failure to recognize that you are not secure, is mainly because you do not have a high degree of emotional self-awareness to notice that you are not processing your emotions, but instead, burying them or pushing them away.

Since you struggle to make yourself consciously aware of your emotional needs, and how your behavior impact others; this makes it difficult to admit that you need help. You experience great discomfort with being vulnerable and this discomfort prevents you from accepting your shortcomings and ask for the support you need.

As a child, you learned that emotional needs and emotional expressions were unimportant, and you may have been criticized or shamed when you exhibited any emotional behavior or response. So, you grew up to believe emotional expression was for the weak, because you learned early, that you had to find ways to regulate yourself – as nobody else would help you do that.

Most individuals with this attachment style will suffer in silence, rather than embrace vulnerability and ask for help.

HOW THE DISMISSIVE AVOIDANT ATTACHED INDIVIDUAL EXPERIENCE RELATIONSHIPS

1. When you feel yourself developing romantic feelings for your partner – your subconscious beliefs which tells you that relationships cannot be trusted, will always be competing with the feelings you're developing. This can cancel out the positive feelings you begin to feel for them.

2. If you haven't worked on yourself around the subconscious fears you have for relationships – this will become a recurring cycle. You might love your partner deeply – however, you also have deep fears around love – which can serve to cancel out the love you have for them.

3. You consciously fear intimacy and have problem regulating your emotions. You prefer to self-regulate using tasks, pets, activities, or routine; things, activities or individuals that does not require emotional energy, or emotional connection from you.

4. You usually associate feeling of vulnerability, need for affection, or attention from others, as being clingy and you respond with feelings of disgust towards your partner.

5. You are very sensitive to any comment or behavior that makes you feel vulnerable, criticized or shamed. You abhor failure, since when you failed as a child, you were criticized or shamed, or left to feel more alone. Your tendency is to remove yourself from the source of criticism as quickly as possible.

6. You're uncomfortable having deep conversations that require connecting to your emotions. Because your emotional tolerance is shallow, conversations are usually surface level and to the point.

7. Your partners/spouses complain that you are cold, emotionally unavailable and distant. They may verbalize they are left feeling empty, lonely, emotionally and physically separate from you, even when occupying the same space.

8. You try your best not to get too close to anyone or allow anyone to get too close to you, because it harkens back to a time when your caregivers or partners would get close, then abandon you. As a result, they learned to withhold emotions because you felt it was not safe to express them.

9. You don't like to depend on anyone to meet your needs. Especially those close to you like your partners/spouse. You believe you might not recover if they disappointed you, and your expectations were dashed.

10. You may randomly bring up past relationships – "the one who got away" to your partner/spouse, as a strategy for distancing, to keep you at a distance and have your partner/spouse constantly wondering about the status of their relationship with you.

11. You are uncomfortable with conversations about commitment, and will distance if your partner brings them up. These conversations make you feel trapped.

12. Your feelings will always be balanced around your subconscious fears of what relationships mean to you, and will be seen through the lens of how you felt abandoned as a child. For example, the inability to trust others and feelings of aloneness, which you have come to embrace and reclassify as independence.

THE DISMISSIVE AVOIDANT PARTNER AFTER A BREAKUP

1. Can shut down or become passive/aggressive to see if they can get a reaction from you. Will use deactivating activities as reason why the relationship wouldn't have worked out anyway.

2. Usually rebounds quickly to get reprieve from pain of breakup and to stifle abandonment wounds they experienced as a child. Although they will never admit it – they do feel pain after a breakup – they just believe it is weak to show it.

3. Will use activities such as long working hours, one-night stands, pornography, smoking, drinking, drugs, dangerous hobbies such as rock climbing etc., to repress pain and take attention from the pain they feel.

4. If breakup was because they felt they could not make you happy, as a result of constant criticism – they are more likely to feel relief, since their self-esteem is tied to their ability to perform at a high level in all that they do. This hearkens back to their childhood when the only time they got any type of attention or validation was when they performed a task well.

5. Months may pass before they actually begin to come to any type of recognition about the loss of a relationship. This is because of their tendency to process emotions very slowly.

6. They may attempt to reconcile if they recognize they may have been a big part of the reason for the breakup. If accepted, they will come back with full gusto and give you all the things you've always asked for – however, this will be short-lived if they do not do the work of healing their attachment style. Don't expect any heartfelt apologies. Any attempt of apology will be in the tasks (acts of service) they do for you; or fulfilling some request you've always wanted them to fulfill.

7. May devalue relationship as a way of coping with a breakup; or may fill time with work, a hobby or other activities that does not require emotional energy from them, to distract from the pain of the breakup.

CHALLENGES OF CHANGE

For the Dismissive Avoidant Attachment Style Individual

As a child, you learned to bury your need for affection so deeply, that now as an adult, you find it extremely difficult to connect why you behave the way they do. Trauma wounds are usually so deeply buried that you struggle to become aware of why you consistently continue to have difficulty in relationships.

In fact, although you know at a superficial level that your parents or caregivers showed you no affection as a child, you often defend your upbringing by saying the way you were treated by your caregivers, enabled and prepared you for a world that can be extremely harsh.

You see your independence and ability to be alone without the need for others, as strength, especially when compared to the anxious preoccupied attachment style, who fears being alone and consistently seek out relationships.

As someone with Dismissive Avoidant attachment style, you most likely find it difficult to connect with your emotions, and is the least likely of the attachment styles to recognize your behavior as a problem and seek help. This is because you lack the emotional capacity or emotional intelligence to delve deep into what may have caused you to respond in relationships the way they have.

You also have the tendency to use your wounds as an excuse to validate the ways in which they behave. For example: your core wound of feeling unworthy of love, formed as a result of your caregiver's failure to give you the emotional and physical connection you asked, to feel worthy of love. You will use this as an excuse to say the love you did not receive, made you stronger and more independent, so you never need to feel dependent on others.

A few reasons you may have chosen to break toxic behavioral patterns may be as a result of extreme emotional pain.

Perhaps after yet another breakup of a relationship with someone, who you believed really loved you, and who you believed you really loved; you've become tired of the recurring themes of behavior which plays out in every one of your relationships. Something inside you recognizes that you are the common denominator in these failed relationships, and you're beginning to realize that you have some work to do on yourself or face the painful fact, that you've never really allowed the experience of true love to blossom in your life, because of all the traumas you experienced as a child.

You've come to the realization that, if you resist changing long enough, something will happen in your life that will put you in a position where you have NO CHOICE - but to change.

As a result of this extreme emotional pain, you may make the difficult decision to finally face your past. You've heard some of the complaints of those you were in relationship with – and they all seem to say the same thing. However, you've chosen to see them as problems other people have, which is not a problem for you. You tell yourself that these individuals are just needy and clingy, and just too emotional. This is indeed quite possible, but when you can recognize your role in their need to be clingy and needy, you may recognize that perhaps if you attended to their emotional needs, they might not have been so needy. When you embrace awareness, and can now see things more clearly, you may begin to question why so many individuals who've never even met each other, always had the same things to say. Can everyone be lying?

Because you're smart, you begin to come to terms that there are things you need to change. You begin the work – knowing that every day you will need to face the traumas of your past, before you can move into your future. You may recognize that there's a part of you that doesn't really want to change and that scares you. You have to come to a place where you can be honest with yourself about what needs to change and why.

_____

_____

_____

_____

_____

On the other hand, some reason why you may have avoided change so far could be that you really didn't see the need to change because you fear change. Since you're not particularly fond of change, you may have wondered if the challenge of creating this change may even be worth it.

It could also be that you're benefiting from your problem in some way. Perhaps it allowed you to hide behind the façade of "independence" so others look up to you for not needing anyone.

THE ROAD TO HEALING

The Following Exercises are Meant to Address Some of the Challenges the Dismissive Avoidant Attachmnent Style Individual May Have in Their Relationships.

EXERCISE 1
BECOMING AWARE OF YOUR CORE WOUNDS AND YOUR SUBCONSCIOUS PATTERNS OF BEHAVIOR

Become aware of how you respond when you:

1. Feel Abandoned
2. Become Emotionally Overwhelmed
3. Feel You Cannot Depend on Anyone
4. You Cannot Trust Anyone to Take Care of Your Needs

With every new awareness – you MUST first question if the thought that brought on the behavior is true. Because you've always acted from a subconscious patterning all your life – you're still using old patterns of behavior to respond to new situations that you may now have autonomy and control over.

These old patterns of behavior began as a way of protecting yourself as a child. Perhaps when your caregivers criticized or rebuffed your bids for emotional connection; you retreated to your room and played some games or played with your toys.

This habitual way of responding to criticism or rejection from your caregivers were habits that calmed you. After responding repetitively in this way for many years, these habits become hard-wired into the subconscious, and now as an adult, this is the way you now respond in your adult relationships.

Let's take a look at habits, what they are, how they are formed and how to break them.

EXERCISE 2:
UNDERSTANDING & OVERCOMING THE FEAR OF CHANGE

As you've read earlier, one of the challenges for your attachment style is the fear of change. Routine gives you a false sense of control over your life, and that is something you developed as a child to feel safer in a world where you could not trust your caregivers to be there for you.

Each of you may be at a different place in your fear of change. Remember that I mentioned earlier that everything always falls along a spectrum. Each of us had different experiences as a child, and we also differ in how we chose to cope with our specific traumas.

By now, you should be paying attention to your thoughts, emotions, and the resulting behavior or response each engenders.

The next step is to learn to identify where you may be stuck in the cycle of creating change.

To assist you with this, here are some tangible ways for you to identify the emotion of fear, and the different ways you may experience them.

This practice is especially integral for the dismissive avoidant because of the challenge you have connecting with your emotions.

Some stages of fear you may encounter on your journey to healing and becoming a more secure individual.

1. **Discomfort/Agitation** — Something about the process of connecting with your emotions, makes you very uncomfortable.

   This growing agitation of the unknown makes you extremely uncomfortable. You attempt to tolerate, repress, ignore this feeling, (as you did when you were a child) but it continues to rear its ugly head when you least expect it.

   You may try to negotiate with yourself that it might be better just dealing with the challenges you've already become accustomed to. Hopefully you will also recognize that, now that you're an adult, with the autonomy to create the change you need — it is now up to you to make that decision to do whatever is required to get the results you need, so you can begin to have more healthy and secure relationships.

2. **Feeling of Overwhelm** — You may begin to feel a sense of overwhelm, at the journey that lies ahead of you. You may feel physically and emotionally exhausted. Hang in there!

   Remember that any new task will take time to adjust to. This is **NOT** the time to give up on yourself. Doing this will only perpetuate the fear of abandonment you felt as a child. You cannot afford to abandon yourself now!

   Enough is Enough - You recognize that if you do not make a change now, that you'll be living the rest of your life with these unhealed traumas that wreak havoc in your relationships. You decide it's time for a change and you take the first step toward change. You feel a sense of hope and you promise yourself you will get the help you need to make these changes. You accept that it won't be easy – but it will be worth it.

3. **Fear Is Always Present** – Recognize that fear does not magically go away when you begin your journey to healing. Expect it, so that you're not surprised when it rears its ugly head.

   Healing is a process, and process takes time. Acknowledge the fear when it comes. Accept that you are experiencing it. Have a conversation with it; "Yes it's uncomfortable, but it's normal to feel this way when I try something new". As long as you don't continue to focus on it, it will pass unceremoniously out of your thoughts.

   Focus instead on the journey at hand. Just keep going and promise yourself never to give up. You may become uncomfortable and anxious throughout this journey. You may doubt your decision. This is just par for the course. Keep going!

4. **You May Want to Retreat:** You May Develop Amnesia around Your Past Challenges – Fear can make you want to retreat to the comfort of old habits. The fear of change can grow strong enough that it makes your past challenges seem much better than you originally thought. You perceive the original situation as less anxiety-producing than the change. You're used to it; it's comfortable; it's familiar. Plus, it has become part of your identity, so you may resist letting it go. You may temporarily forget why you wanted to change so badly.

   This is normal! Our brains are designed to keep us safe. It's how it protects us from harm. Anything out of the ordinary –

trying something new which brings discomfort, will generate feelings of fear by our brain.

Because every thought you think is not true; this is when you should ask these questions to get you back on track, "Is what I'm currently doing harmful to me; will it kill me? What can I expect if I continue down this path of change? What evidence do I have that my past way of being in relationships was unhealthy?"

If you answer these questions correctly; "Is what I'm currently doing harmful to me – will it kill me? No, it's not harmful. It is uncomfortable, but it won't kill me.

"What can I expect if I continue down this path?" Well, I can expect to become more secure so I can begin to have healthy, happy relationships.

"What evidence do I have that my past way of being in relationships was not healthy?"

I think you got this one. Just try to remember all the experiences you had in your past relationships, and how the ways you showed up in relationships, also negatively affected your partners.

5. **Backtracking** — Understand that this is a possibility. Most people slip back into old patterns of behavior. We are ALL human and we make mistakes and we don't always make the right decisions. Learn from this setback, and understand that it's all that it is – a setback.

Get up! Brush yourself off! And start again!

EXERCISE 3:
DISTURBING ENTRENCHED HABITS BY UNDERSTANDING HOW THESE SUBSONSCIOUS PATTERNS OF BEHAVIOR FORMED & HOW TO BREAK THEM

Habits are behavior patterns that are regularly practiced until they become involuntary. There are of course, harmful and harmless habits, and it's the harmful habits that can wreak havoc in our lives that I will be focused on in this book.

Habits first begins as a choice that is deliberately made at some point. However, when practiced day after day, these choices became habitual and hard-wired into the subconscious.

After some time, this individual now reacts to triggers from their past in automatic ways; many times, without even recognizing it.

It is only when you become aware of your subconscious patterns of behavior that you will finally be able to make changes to them.

What thoughts, behaviors, (triggers) causes you to react in a certain way. How do you normally respond for each trigger? What is a better way to respond? Finally, you make changes by replacing old toxic patterns with new healthy patterns of behavior.

I have a habit of sitting cross-legged when in a relaxed environment – home, with friends, family. I don't remember how it began, but now I do it without even realizing that I'm doing it. Some individuals wipe their utensils before using them, especially when dining in a restaurant. These are habits that can be categorized as harmless.

Brushing our teeth when we get up in the mornings can be categorized as a good habit; however, we all have those habits that can be categorized as harmful or "bad" because they tend to make our lives miserable.

Since we're focused on the dismissive avoidant attached individual in this book, let's examine some of the habits – usually subconscious – that now as adults, cause a myriad of unhealthy patterns of behaviors in this individual.

Since this individual could not depend on their caregivers for emotional connection or validation, they learned early that they had to find ways to provide that for themselves.

Perhaps as children they soothe themselves by playing with their toys – now as adults, they may use excessive gaming, high-risk activities (one-night stands, jumping off cliffs, sky-diving, fast driving, long hours at work, excessive cleaning, collecting inanimate objects) to soothe themselves.

These activities allowed them to get away from the people who rejected them, while connecting them to activities that does not require the emotional connection they did not get from their caregivers.

EXERCISE 4:
REPLACING TOXIC PATTERNS WITH NEW HEALTHY PATTERNS OF BEHAVIOR

The goal here is to reprogram the subconscious – just like it was programed when you were a child. This is done through repetition, with emotions and consistency.

One way to begin changing those toxic patterns is to, for example, instead of watching pornography – watch a documentary, travel channel, read a book, go for a walk, exercise.

Instead of working overtime – do some of the chores around the home and ask someone to help you with them – your partner or children. This will also help promote and build your emotional muscle of connection while doing things together with those close to you.

EXERCISE 5:
GETTING COMFORTABLE WITH ASKING FOR HELP

This will allow you to work on the trauma you have around asking for help and trusting others to be there for you. There is one caveat:

Please be sure this person truly wants to work to help you do this. Remind them it may be challenging, but if this person chose to stay with you despite the difficulty of the relationship, I believe you're good to go.

1. Let your partner know what you are trying to do. Ask them for their help, patience and support during this process.
2. Pay attention to you respond to your partner – until now you probably responded without thinking how your response is affecting your partner or anyone else.
3. Practice sitting in a place of discomfort and realize that you WILL NOT DIE even if it feels that way.
4. Do 1 thing each day that is uncomfortable for you – give a heartfelt compliment – listen to a concern your partner has without trying to fix it (just listen and attempt to understand the emotions he/she's sharing). Really listen – practice to allow your feelings to create the empathy that others need from you – accept their empathy. Before you isolate yourself; question your response to the situation – ask yourself questions – Is what I'm feeling logical? True? Makes Sense? What would I need to be thinking to believe this is true about this situation? Could there be a different explanation or answer to this question?

5. Practice focusing on what is right and good in your relationship and in your life. Write it down and make a gratitude list to use before bed and on arising. What are you grateful about (your partner/spouse, your job, your family, health, etc.,). Write a list of the things you love about your partner. Focus on the good.

6. Take art classes or listen to some classical music. These art forms activate the right side of the brain that is responsible for emotional expression. Try to connect with the mood of the different instruments. This will put you in touch with your emotional side. Do this as often as possible.

7. Do mindful exercises – pay attention to something (your breathing, a plant swaying in the wind, the ticking of the hands of a clock, anything you enjoy observing that will stay constant for the time you plan to observe it). Take in all the features of the activity or object without any distractions from your phone or other people. This means you have to find a quiet place to practice this until you're able to focus completely on something, even when there are distractions around you.

8. Make eye contact with your partner for short periods and see if you can identify their mood. If you're working with your partner/spouse, ask them if you identify their mood correctly.

9. Listen to your partner's concerns and try not to rush them. Ask clarifying questions (do this for short periods of time, until you build up the emotional muscles to have longer conversations).

10. Watch movies together or apart, which require emotional connection - notice the expressions on the actor's faces etc.

If you're with your partner, notice the emotions on his/her face and try to understand why they feel that emotion. Try to lean into the emotions of your partner and the actors on the screen. (Movie example: Beautiful Boy).

EXERCISE 6:
FORGIVENESS - THE RELEASE

This step is usually the first step to healing for other attachment styles. However, because of the disconnection the dismissive avoidant experiences with their emotions; this step comes AFTER healing begins and the individual begins to connect with their emotions.

When he/she is able to unearth the buried emotions of their past and is now able to allow themselves to become vulnerable in expressing them; it is now time to begin to forgive those you now clearly recognize were participants in causing the development of your particular attachment style.

This style has for years led you to participate in certain behaviors that have been the cause of great pain and emotional injury to many.

Perhaps as this reality becomes evident, you may begin to feel a lot of guilt and shame for how you behaved in prior relationships.

You are now ready the journey to forgive your caregivers and yourself, first, recognizing that your caregivers may not have known how to nurture children and was perhaps just caring for you in the same way in which they were cared for as children, and neither were you aware of the pain and injury you have caused in your past relationships.

Sometimes it is evident that the caregivers knew exactly how much they were harming you as a child; as in cases of sexual molestation, physical and emotional abuse, and cruel acts of rejection.

In these cases, you must find it in your heart somewhere to forgive them. Otherwise, the pain of resentment and sometimes, pure hate, can eat you up inside.

This is not an easy task, however, when you recognize that there is nothing you can do to change your past, and that forgiving others does not mean you allow them back in your life to harm you all over again. When you can recognize that your healing can only truly begin when you cast off the very heavy baggage of hate and pain, only then will you be able to move forward and heal.

The individual you need to forgive does not need to be with you, or to apologize to you in order to forgive them. Forgiving them is to free you from the bondage of hate and resentment which serves to hold you hostage to your past.

Forgiveness Exercise: The How

This exercise is necessary to move on from the hurt and pain you have experienced in the past, and which may be still holding you hostage to bitterness, resentment, regret, and anger. It is imperative to get this resolved before you can heal: and healing is necessary before you can move forward with our lives.

Forgiveness is for you – not the other person.

Forgiveness does not mean you forget the wrongs done to you, or that the other person has accepted responsibility for the pain they caused you.

Forgiveness frees you from the bitterness and pain that holding onto unforgiveness brings.

While the other person is going on with their lives – you remain stuck and connected to them because you refuse to let it go. Forgiveness frees you to move on with your life, without the baggage of negativity and bitterness and resentment you carried around for so long.

Steps

1. Write on **loose paper** the names of all the people who hurt you or caused you pain. **DON'T FORGET TO ADD YOURSELF TO THE LIST**
2. We all have things we blame ourselves for. (Perhaps you blamed yourself for not being able to defend your mom from abuse). Realize that you were just a child and had no power to do so.
3. Write a list of what they said, didn't say; did, didn't do; to hurt you.
4. Do this for everyone on your list from as far back as you can remember. Take your time. There is no rush.
5. When you're finished, go over the list again. Read it slowly, allowing yourself to feel the pain and whatever emotions that come up for each incident.
6. Cry and allow the pain to wash all over you. (You must go THROUGH it before you can come out the other side and begin to heal).
7. When you're done, go over the list again. This time – pretending the person is sitting in a chair across from you.

You tell them how much they hurt you, give specific examples that come to mind. When you're satisfied that you emptied yourself of all the hurt you've carried for so long – close your eyes and relax by breathing in and out – slowly – about 3 times. When you feel relaxed, say to them, "YOU'VE HURT ME FOR SO LONG. I NOW RECOGNIZE THAT I WAS THE ONE SUFFERING BECAUSE I DIDN'T WANT TO FORGIVE YOU. TODAY, I'M TAKING BACK THE POWER I GAVE YOU OVER ME. SO - I FORGIVE YOU AND LET YOU GO, SO I CAN FINALLY BE FREE TO GO ON WITH MY LIFE."

8. When you are finished – get some matches and a large container that is safe to burn the paper on which these memories were written.

9. Burn each leaf of paper and as you do – say, "This chapter of my life is over. I am moving on with the life I deserve. I forgive you and let you go."

10. Take the ashes from the sheets of paper and find a place to bury it in the soil.

   YOU'RE HOLDING A FUNERAL FOR ALL THE CAUSES OF THE BITTERNESS AND PAIN YOU'VE BEEN HOLDING ONTO FOR SO LONG.

11. When you've buried the ashes: Say, "I am now free to live my best life. I have so much to offer and so much good to experience. I am ready. It is TIME!

EXERCISE 7:
IDENTIFYING EMOTIONS & BEHAVIORAL RESPONSE

Controlling our emotions is an extremely important skill. We just have to look around us to see evidence of the horrible results that "lack of self-control" can cause.

So many individuals have difficulty identifying their emotions, however, when it comes to the different attachment styles, the dismissive avoidant might be the most challenged in this area.

Some reasons for this may be:

- As a child, you were made to believe your feelings did not matter

- Your caregivers did not encourage emotional expressions. As an adult, you now find emotional expressions extremely uncomfortable.

- You were made to feel guilty for expressing your emotions (or desires) as they might have been an inconvenience to others.

- You were discouraged, shamed and criticized for feeling or expressing specific emotions. This chronic rejection of emotional expression usually results in stunted ability to recognize emotions and the resulting feelings.

In order to re-gain your power of autonomy to manage your own emotional state, you need to be able to:

- Notice when you're experiencing an emotion and identify what it is.

- Learn how to change your emotional state (that is, the thoughts, and the emotions you experienced as a result of the meaning you give to the thought). Our emotions occur as a result of the interpretations we make of these experiences (usually expressed by our thoughts), and the meanings we give them.

There are many opportunities between thought and behavior, where we can make changes, which will determine the end result.

It works like this:

First, we have a stimuli or trigger.

Your usual way of responding to this stimuli/trigger was from a subconscious place, where you discern the stimuli/trigger and you react in a preconceived way, as it relates to your prior experiences – repeated over and over again. Because this learned way of responding was repeated over and over again, perhaps for many years, the brain no longer uses valuable energy to process it.

This constant repetitive though pattern (meaning given to thought) was performed so often, that it became hard-wired into the subconscious and now, as soon as a similar stimuli/trigger makes its appearance – next thing you know, you're reacting in the exact same way you've always done, so many times before.

As I mentioned earlier, there are many opportunities to break that pattern if you know where they are.

So, let's see how this works.

Remember that stimuli/trigger? When that enters your consciousness as a thought, you give a meaning to the thought. The meaning that you give, is usually one you've been giving that stimuli/trigger for many years. The meaning you give a thought will determine which emotion it brings forward. The emotion that is brought forward, is what will determine your response (behavior or words).

Let's go back to the meaning we give to the stimuli/trigger, since it is at this juncture that we can choose to make changes to the meanings we give to the thought. Remember that it is the meaning we give to the thought, that will determine the resulting behavior. So, if we change the meaning to a more positive one, we will begin to interrupt the existing pattern of behavior and begin to form new patterns.

This cannot be a one and done deal though. You will need to change the meanings every time you get triggered. The more often this is done, the quicker the new pattern of behavior will emerge.

After a while, this new pattern becomes the norm of how you now respond to your past triggers/stimuli.

The old patterns will not magically go away, but now, you easily recognize your triggers and you know how to respond (change the meaning) to get a better result.

Let's examine a scenario as an example.

As a child, your parents beat you often with a leather belt. Now as an adult, you see someone pulling their leather belt from their waist and even though this may be a total stranger, and you're now an adult, the stimuli/trigger of seeing a belt being removed, causes you to become very uncomfortable. If you've never connected the reasons why you feel this way, you may wonder why you get this feeling of dread around this action.

This happens because the fear of this moment was buried in your subconscious as a child, and when done often enough, can create a lot of fear and dread which got stored in your body.

Back to the belt example.

So now you're an adult and you see the same scenario being played out, as it did when you were a child. Immediately your subconscious mind connects to the leather belt to the beatings you got as a child.

Now here's where you can change the meaning.

Ask yourself these questions:

Is this person getting ready to harm me? "Nope"

And if they were, am I now able to defend myself? "Yes"

What else could be happening here? "This person may have just eaten too much and has chosen to remove his/her belt, so that he/she can feel more comfortable".

This meaning will result in a totally new emotion – instead of fear and dread, it could be laughter and fun.

EXERCISE 8:
RECOGNIZE COMMON EMOTIONS IN OTHERS

Below I will describe some common emotions, what they look like, and how they may be expressed.

These descriptions will help you get a general idea of the signs and behavioral expressions of each emotion to make them easier to identify.

You may be wondering why this is necessary. Unfortunately for someone with the dismissive avoidant attachment style, emotional expressions, or understanding them in others, is somewhat of a challenge. However, this is extremely important on your way to becoming more secure, since the earlier you're able to identify your emotions; the more successful you will be at managing them.

Please remember that everyone's experiences each emotion somewhat differently – along a spectrum - and you may not experience all of the characteristics described.

Happiness: (emotion)

When someone is happy, there is an intense positive feeling of pleasure, feeling of contentment, expressions of joy, delight and wellbeing.

You hold your head high, you smile and laugh a lot, muscles are relaxed, and your body language is open and inviting. Your voice is pleasant, friendly, arms swing easily as you walk, there is a bounce to your step and you feel like dancing.

Boredom (emotion)

You feel down and unmotivated, unpleasant feelings of indifference, restlessness, emptiness, and frustration is the norm. You see only the bad in everything.

Yor energy is low and you walk around in a slumped posture. Eyes are dull and lifeless, and you walk around with a frown or look of dejection. Your breathing is shallow and you fidget a lot. Sometimes you may find yourself just staring off into space.

Fear (emotion)

You may have unpleasant feelings of dread or impending doom, uneasiness, stress, apprehension, and nervousness. You are flooded with thoughts of uncertainty and worry, racing thoughts, difficulty concentrating and remembering and this happens because you live in the past or the future where you have no power to make changes or control things. As a result, you live with a sense of helplessness and hopelessness.

You experience bouts of sweating, clammy hands, hunched shoulders, quickened shallow breath, eyes darting back and forth, butterflies in the stomach, light headedness and nausea.

You continually pace back and forth, biting your lip and fidgeting. You are hypervigilant of your surroundings.

Anger (emotion)

You experience intense feelings of hostility and hurt. You feeling out of control and thoughts of blame and resentment prevents you from thinking clearly or rationally. Your muscles are tensed up, and you may experience headaches, a tight chest, increased heart rate, and increased blood pressure. Your breathing is heavy.

Other outer expressions can be, a clenched fist, furrowed brow, showing teeth, clenched jaw, sweating, trembling, flushed cheeks, large posture (as when ready to attack). Voice is usually loud, with a lot of shouting, cursing and sarcasm. You pace (similar to a caged animal).

Acts of aggression can include hitting a wall, throwing objects, among others.

Sadness (emotion)

You may feel intense pain and sorrow, unworthiness, disappointment, helplessness, gloominess, grief, numbness, loss of interest and no hope for the future.

You feel defeated and may have difficulty concentrating and remembering. Your posture is slumped and your shoulders hunched. Your eyes look lifeless, and may show signs of prolonged crying.

You walk slowly and your voice is monotone in monotone. You may curl up into a ball, when you sleep and you withdraw from those around you.

EXERCISE 9:
COMMUNICATING WITH EMPATHY

Empathetic listening requires that we pay attention to others by identifying their emotional state.

To express empathy, we need to really listen to what the individual has to say. This requires "active listening" which is paraphrasing what the the person said, to make sure we understand what they really mean.

Empathetic listening occurs when you ask questions about how the person feels about the situation. Empathetic listening requires that you really stay in tune with another. An empathetic response might be, "I can see how this has upset you. Do you want to talk about it?"

Sympathy vs. Empathy

Empathy is not sympathy. Whereas sympathy is "feeling sorry for someone," empathy is "putting yourself in the place of someone and feeling as they feel, (without judgement) if you were in their place."

To truly empathize, you must take on the perspective of the other person – not your own.

Some qualities of being empathetic are:

1. Give them your undivided attention.
2. Resist the urge to be judgmental and try not to minimize or trivialize the individual's issue.

3. Try to read the speaker's emotional state. Observe the emotions behind the words.

   Do they look sad, afraid, hopeless, angry, afraid, frustrated, resistant, or resentful? Respond to the emotion as well as the words.

4. It's okay not to have the answer to everything. Get comfortable with silence so you can allow them to express themselves.

5. Ask clarifying questions and restate what you perceive your partner is saying AND, specifically, feeling.

EXERCISE 10:
HOW TO IDENTIFY YOUR & YOUR ROMANTIC PARTNER'S LOVE LANGUAGE

This section will use content from Gary Chapman's book, "The 5 Love Languages" to introduce you to 5 ways we express love in our relationships.

For the dismissive avoidant, this particular aspect of relationships produces a real challenge.

I cannot tell you the number of conversations I've had with client's whose romantic partners/spouses, with an anxious preoccupied/ambivalent attachment style, have literally cried as they shared how lonely and unloved, they feel in their relationships.

These patterns happen all too frequently in relationships between the dismissive avoidant and the anxious pre-occupied attachment style individuals, are like magnets for each other.

In order to make it simple to understand these love languages; I will give examples of what these can look like to make it more tangible.

Note: One important thing to remember, is that the way **you** feel loved, might be quite different from the way your partner/spouse feels loved. Pay attention to what makes your partner "light up" – not what **you** feel good doing for him/her.

Here's an example.

I remember hearing from one of my female clients.

"He keeps fixing everything (acts of service) around the house all weekend; when all I want is for him to take some time off to spend time with me or just cuddling and watching TV with me.

The husband was upset that his wife would complain about him fixing stuff around the house. He felt that "cuddling" (personal touch) and spending time (quality time) was meaningless – except for the fact that, "cuddling and spending time" with his wife was what made her feel loved.

Words of Affirmation

1. You love to hear your partner say, "I love you." Those three words are particularly meaningful, special, and reassuring for you to hear. You never tire of hearing those 3 words.
2. You like to be appreciated and acknowledged for the things you do. It's nice to know your efforts are recognized with kind words, no matter how small it is. It makes you feel valued and loved.
3. When your partner notices the new dress you're wearing – it magical. Maybe it's a new hair style or color. It shows they are paying attention to you, which helps you feel valued and cherished.
4. You feel special when they take the time to bring up a memory of a special day or time you spent together.
5. When you do something nice for your partner, they always say, "Thank you." This makes you feel recognized and valued and not taken for granted.

Quality Time

1. It means a lot to you when your partner makes time for you, prioritize you in their schedule, and rarely cancel plans.
2. You cherish uninterrupted time with your partner. It's a priority for you spend time together, hanging out and enjoying each other, both of you giving each other your focused attention. It means a lot to you to create new memories and sharing new experiences with your partner.
3. You relish time spent together with your partner, and you feel content and happy when you're together - even when doing the usual mundane task of each day. The important thing for you is the time you spend together.

Acts of Services

1. You feel supported and taken care of when your partner helps lessen the workload.
2. You feel cared for when your partner notices when you need help and jumps in without you having to ask. It shows that they were paying attention and you feel special when your partner pays attention to the little details of your life.
3. You value action over words. You need someone you can rely on to do what they say they will do. It doesn't have to be a big "to do" to make you feel special. Little things can mean a lot.

Gifts

1. You feel loved when you receive a gift. The gift itself is nice, but what matters most to you, is the fact that they thought about you, and tool the time to select a gift they know you

would love. The gift itself is just a tangible representation of the love your partner has for you.

2. The gift does not have to be bought in a store, it could be something you took the time to make, just for your partner. A playlist of their favorite songs, a unique, stone or shell from a beach you visited, something you painted just for them, etc.,

3. Receiving a gift demonstrates that you are valued, cared for, and loved.

Physical Touch

1. You look forward to hugs, cuddles, and kissing. Nothing beats tactile, physical intimacy. Sexual intimacy makes you feel loved and closer to your partner.

2. You feel secure in a relationship when physical affection is mutual. You enjoy holding hands, long embraces, and kisses and you're comfortable with public displays of affection. It makes you feel wanted and desired.

3. If your partner is sitting next to you, you would rather sit side-to-side and cuddle up. The closer, the better. If they are nearby, it's almost automatic you reach out to them to touch their leg, play with their hair, or give them a back rub.

Please remember that not all of these will be embraced by individuals from different cultural backgrounds. For example, the British are not very comfortable with public displays of affection, while for some European cultures (Italians, Spanish) hugs and kisses in public are the norm.

IN CLOSING

I hope I've managed to give you enough information on how to identify the dismissive avoidant attachment style individual, some of the challenges they face in their relationships, and finally, some tools (exercises) to help move you to a more secure way of experiencing relationships.

Or perhaps, you're the partner/spouse of someone with this attachment style. If so, I also hope this was helpful for you to understand why your partner responds the way he/she does in your relationship, and how you may be able to work together (if your partner chooses) to have a healthier relationship, moving forward.

Please visit my YouTube Channel to learn more about attachment styles and other lifechanging tools. Please feel free to reach out to me if you need one-on-one or couple's relationship or life coaching. Email address is available in description below each video. Thank you!

Made in United States
North Haven, CT
15 September 2023

41600251R00048